B

Book Three

Bears in Love Series

PA Vachon

© 2018 by PA Vachon

ISBN: 978-1986189651

Dedication

To the ladies of P.A.'s BearsandBabes, you are all amazing and don't let anyone tell you any different. To my grandparents, who nurtured my love of all things happily ever after. To Jules, you are an amazing cheerleader. Thank you for always talking me off the ledge. To my editor Summer, you are still awesome and a great sounding board.

And as always, to my life, my love, my one. You are my everything, forever…

"Though I saw it coming, it still hurts..."

Prologue
~Regan~

Winter 2 years earlier...

Regan Jensen knew in her heart that she would do whatever it took to protect the unborn cub in her womb. She was going to be a mom. It wasn't ever one of the things she'd dreamed of as a child. Her own mother had passed away the year she turned eleven. She missed all of those important mother daughter milestones. Instead she had her dad, Marcus, who loved her and cared for her but when it came to girl things, he was clueless. Those were some rough years. Luckily, one of the older female members of the clan had taken Regan into town when she needed a bra, when that dreaded time of the month had started, and again when she was old enough to start thinking about sex. Condoms were a must... No baby for a teenage clan princess. Her dad was going to shit a brick when he found out he was going to be a grandpa. She was an unmated twenty year old clan princess. This was craptastic.

Regan watched as David made his way to their spot, a small pond just up the road from the family compound. It was such a peaceful place, lush and green in the spring and summer. The perfect place to spend time with your mate, even if he refused to claim you. The soft grass was a wonderful place for an afternoon of lovemaking. That's what it was, lovemaking. They weren't fucking or just having sex... They loved each other. Or at least she loved David and she thought he loved her too. But you can't always have everything that you want. Sometimes life gets in the way. This conversation was not going to be pleasant but it was something that they had to talk about. David still didn't know about the life she had growing inside of her, their little miracle. Their cub. So far she had been able to hide it from everyone. She didn't have much time though. She was leaving on a Secret Keeper mission the next day. She still hadn't told David about the Secret Keepers, the enforcers for the shifter community. The enforcers and their clan of grizzlies had been fighting with Hatchet, a maniac leader of a clan of black bears that were too close to exposing their secrets. They were sometimes judge, jury and executioner in certain situations.

"Babe," David smiled at her, "I'm glad you're here. We need to talk."

"I know we do," she sighed heavily, not really prepared for their upcoming discussion.

"Regan, it will be fine," he replied. "You'll see."

"It won't be though," she murmured.

"I know you think that it won't," David said, "but I promise you, we'll be together soon."

"We can't be together if you won't leave that psychotic clan of bears," she said, raising her voice in frustration. This wasn't the first time they'd had this particular discussion.

"Regan, you have to trust me," David said.

"David, you're my mate, and I trust you," Regan said, "but mate or not, I can't break our laws."

"I know, baby," David sighed out, "but I have to stay and see this through."

"You don't have to be a part of a rogue clan," she replied. "I'll talk to my father. He'll let you join us. Especially since we're mates. He would never make us stay apart."

"I just can't," David said again.

Regan looked at David sadly, not understanding why he insisted on being a part of Hatchet's clan.

It was insanity. Those bears were going to get their species discovered. No matter what she said, he refused, and she wouldn't tell him about the cub just to get her way. She couldn't manipulate him in that way. He needed to want to stay for them, not just because a small life was joining their world in just over six months. They were both shifters, so the pregnancy would be more like a grizzly than a human.

"David, I need you to join me with my father," she begged and she didn't typically beg. "I can't be with you if you're against our most sacred of laws.

"I'm sorry, Regan," David replied. "I can't leave them."

"Then I can't do this with you anymore," she said as she cried silently, tears leaving wet tracks on her cheeks.

Regan turned away to leave. Walking quickly back to her small Honda, she got in the driver's seat, wiped her eyes, and started the car. The engine came to life with a small growl, like a squirrel protecting its horde. As she drove away, she turned on the radio. Much to her chagrin, Sara Evans 'A Little Bit Stronger' was just starting. She sang along as she let the tears flow, knowing that this was it. No mate, no love. Just a product of their time together quickly becoming a reality.

Regan pulled into the compound and turned off the engine. Wiping her face one last time, she got out of her car and started to walk towards her father, Marcus, to let him know about his grandchild.

Instead of leaving the next day on her mission, she was sent out early on an emergency mission that would keep her away from home for almost her entire pregnancy, tracking a rogue wolf through the Olympic National Forest. Luckily, he found a pack to take him in and set him on the right path, so her services as an enforcer were not needed, except as surveillance.

"I want to get so drunk I never remember you again..."

Chapter Two

~ David~

As she walked away, David was having an internal argument with himself. His grizzly didn't understand that he had to stay with Hatchet's clan. He only wanted to be with their mate. Unbeknownst to Regan, his name wasn't even David. It was Johnny. It was killing him to watch her leave, but it was for the best. They hadn't claimed each other at this point. It should be easy to walk away. Too bad his bear didn't agree. He was being ripped apart inside by his bear, the anguished roaring and heartache like knives tearing his soul to ribbons.

David stood there in their favorite spot for what seemed like forever. Waiting. For what, he wasn't sure. Maybe for Regan to come back to him, or maybe for his bear to calm down enough so that he could return to Hatchet's clan. He was still here on a mission, no matter that his heart was breaking.

He slowly walked back to the road, got into his car, and drove away, checking the rear view mirror the whole way back to the clan hideout, thinking about his fated mate and hating that he'd had to let her go, but it wasn't forever. Just until this travesty of a clan was brought to justice. The clan was using an old abandoned farm not all that far from where Regan lived with her clan to keep a low profile. He pulled into the overgrown driveway and headed for the dilapidated barn around the back of the listing two story house.

Sounds of someone being hit could be heard coming from inside. As he walked closer to the barn doors, he could also hear someone groan each time a fist or foot hit its target. What he walked into would stay with him for a very long time.

Tied to a middle post, with her clothes hanging off her in tatters, was Lauren, Ian's mate. They were so screwed. You never hurt someone's mate. Especially not a grizzly's mate. Those fuckers were huge, scary, and they didn't ever back down.

"What the fuck?" David yelled as his eyes adjusted to the gloom inside the barn.

"I'll finally have my revenge," Hatchet said. "Those grizzlies won't tell me what I can and can't do."

"Hatchet, I told you this was a bad idea," David began, trying to get him to see sense. It wasn't working at all. He was hell bent on revenge and making Marcus pay, something Johnny still didn't understand and maybe never would.

"Don't be such a pussy, boy," Hatchet yelled in his direction as he sneered down at the woman tied to the center post. "She'll pay for their mistakes, and when they get here, they'll see what we're really capable of."

"I'm not doing this anymore," David replied. "You've gone too far this time." He started towards Hatchet to help Lauren escape when he heard a commotion outside. Looking out through the partially open doors, Johnny could see Ian's Mustang come to a shuddering halt, throwing dust and rock up into the air.

He was done. He couldn't do this anymore. He missed Regan and he wanted to be with her more than he'd wanted to be an Enforcer for the Secret Keepers. He walked away without a backwards glance and went in search of his mate.

It took him two weeks of constant searching to figure out that she had just completely disappeared from the face of the Earth.

Luckily, Ian and Trevor had been able to rescue Lauren and end Hatchet's insanity. Unfortunately, Janet had returned in time to see Ian kill Hatchet, and Johnny had heard through the grapevine that it was just a matter of time before she would go back for revenge. He'd wandered for about six months, his inner animal lost without Regan, wondering if she was still out there and if she was okay.

Once he'd finally stopped wandering, he was given another mission: to attach himself to Janet's side and keep her under surveillance for the time being. Johnny knew it was only a matter of months before she would go back to avenge Hatchet's death. It took closer to eighteen months for her to gather enough reinforcements to go after the grizzly clan.

"Regret, I regret nothing we had..."

Chapter Three

~ Regan ~

I stared down into the sweetest face I'd ever seen, love welling up inside of me and overflowing for my perfect little cub. My Rory. She was now my reason for living. I spent six long months away from the clan, away from my family, never telling any of them that I was pregnant. It was a shitty thing to do to them, but I needed time to heal from my broken heart. My mate didn't love me enough to want to claim me, and I definitely wasn't going to tell him about our cub just to make him stay.

Rory started fussing, rooting around and making small suckling noises. As she latched on, the door opened to allow Lauren access to my hospital room.

"You know, everyone is outside in the waiting room," she said, "waiting to welcome our newest clan member and to welcome you home."

"I know," I replied. "I feel terrible that I didn't tell anyone about Rory before coming home. But I didn't feel that I had any other choice. I wasn't ready to answer the hundred or so questions everyone would have."

"I get that, Regan," Lauren answered. "But you still need to at least let Marcus in to meet his granddaughter."

"I will," I sighed. "I'm not really ready to face my father with my failure. Not Rory but my unplanned pregnancy without a mate in sight."

Lauren turned to leave me in privacy to finish feeding Rory and probably to go and take care of her own sweet babies. I had heard that she had given birth to twin boys just a few weeks prior to my coming home to Fall City. I was so excited for her and Ian and I couldn't wait to meet the boys.

Rory finished feeding, and I had just brought her up to my shoulder to burp her when my father walked in the door with a happy look on his face but disappointment in his eyes. The disappointment is what was nearly my undoing. I could feel the tears trying to escape. I took a big breath in and readied myself for whatever was coming.

"Regan, sweetheart," my dad began, "why didn't you tell me?"

"I don't know, Daddy," I answered as the tears made slow tracks down my cheeks. "I guess I was embarrassed and worried you'd think I'd let you down."

"Baby, you could never let me down," Marcus replied. "I just wish you'd told me. I could have kept you home."

"I needed to go, Dad," I said. "I needed time to myself."

"I know, darling," my dad answered. "You are more like me than you think."

I looked at my dad for the first time without the fog of youth and I could see the lines around his eyes, the wrinkles that were not overly pronounced but still there, and wondered how he had survived after mom had died. David wasn't dead. The pain I went through every day, wishing and waiting for him, I wouldn't want to put on anyone. I watched as our daughter closed her pretty green eyes, stretched out with a full body yawn, and fell into a peaceful sleep.

"I'm going to go and get the cabin ready for you both," Marcus said. "I'll be back tomorrow morning to take my pretty girls home."

I waited for my dad to leave, cuddled my baby girl to me, and let the tears flow. I missed David. I wanted him here to see the miracle we had created. I didn't even know where to start looking for him. Hatchet's old clan had scattered like rats abandoning a sinking ship, leaving no forwarding address or phone number.

I continued to cuddle Rory as I looked out the window, absentmindedly thinking on the best way to find David. If he was still in the area, I might run into him at some point and then I would have to come clean and tell him about our daughter. There was no mistaking who her father was; she had his green eyes and a full shock of blonde colored hair with just a touch of my red. She would break hearts one day. I would do anything to keep her heart safe and protected. I fell asleep with my Rory swaddled in a blanket at my side, thinking of my mate and wondering if he was thinking of me too.

I woke just after 2 o'clock in the morning to a small whimpering sound. My baby girl was hungry and searching for food. As she fed, I watched her in awe and vowed to never leave her side, no matter what happened. Once she was done feeding, we both drifted back to sleep. I didn't wake again until my dad arrived to take us home, back to the compound where I was born and where I would raise my little bit alone.

"Hey, sweet pea, are you girls ready to go home?" Marcus asked.

"Yes, more than ready," I answered, looking up into his eyes. "Thank you for picking us up, Dad."

"I wouldn't have it any other way, sweet pea," he replied, squeezing my hand. He smiled, letting my hand go. He grabbed our bags from the end of the bed.

An orderly arrived with the prerequisite wheelchair to take us to the exit doors. We traveled the hallways slowly, a few minutes' walk seeming to take hours while I sat in the chair being wheeled towards the elevators. Once outside, we thanked the orderly, and I took my little cub and placed her carefully in the rear-facing car seat my dad had gotten from somewhere, most likely the local Walmart. It's a good thing that I took that safety class at our local fire department. These things were like alien spaceships with all the straps, belts, and pillow-like cushions. Once all of the various straps were fastened correctly, I got into the backseat of the truck as well. I didn't want to be any further than arms' reach from my little cub. We left the parking lot of the hospital and turned towards home. No sooner had we left the town limits, Rory was sleeping soundly next to me. I gazed down at her and then looked up in time to see my dad with a goofy grin on his face looking at us in the rear view mirror.

"Dad," I began, "are you mad at me about this whole thing? Rory, I mean, and my pregnancy?"

"Sweet pea, I'm not mad, just like I said yesterday. A little sad that you didn't feel you could talk to me about the baby," he answered. "I could have helped you and made the fool who left stay."

"That's not what I wanted, Dad,' I told him firmly. "I don't want to talk about him, ever." I couldn't help but be protective of my unclaimed mate. I was pissed at him for sure, but he was still the father of my little cub.

"Alright, darling," Dad said. "Don't get your back up. We won't talk about it again. But you need to know that if he comes back, he and I are going to have words."

"I know, Dad," I sighed in exasperation.

We arrived at the compound in record time. My dad helped me get Rory and all of our things into the cabin. When I walked inside, I was glad to be home again. I'd missed the sights, smells, and feeling of home. I missed my clan mates, my dad, and my brothers. I walked further into the living room and saw that a small port-a-crib had been set in one corner. I looked back at my dad and raised an eyebrow.

"Dad, where did that come from?" I asked, while making my way to the far end of the hall to my bedroom door.

"I got it in town yesterday," he answered. "My granddaughter needs a place to nap, doesn't she?"

I laughed a little as I opened my door. When it swung open the rest of the way, I gasped. My dad had added a rocking chair and wooden crib. The crib itself looked like something from a dream, flouncy pink around the bottom like a skirt, a pastel colored blanket, and sheet set with little bear cubs wearing pink bows in their fur. It was the cutest thing I had ever seen.

"Dad," I murmured as the emotion overwhelmed me and I began to silently cry. My dad came up and gathered me into a soothing hug, shushing my tears. He'd always hated to see me cry.

"Darling', I love you and that little cub," Dad stated, "and I want you to stay here as long as you need or want to."

"Thanks, Daddy," I replied.

I wandered closer to the crib and laid Rory on the pink cotton candy cloud. Sighing, I watched as she slept on.

I turned towards my dad and we left the bedroom, leaving the door ajar. We walked into the kitchen and sat at the table.

"Regan, what are you going to do about the Secret Keepers?" My dad asked.

"I'm taking a leave of absence for now," I answered, "until I can decide what I want to do."

"That's a good idea, Bug," my dad said, calling me by my childhood nickname.

"I am going to lay down for a while," I told my dad, "I need to nap when Rory does, according to the nurses and Lauren."

"Ok, Bug," Dad replied. "Love you, and I'll see you when you get up."

I went back down the hall and entered my bedroom, checked on Rory, and then crawled into bed. Once I lay down, I was out like a light. Exhaustion had finally caught up with me. I slept until Rory woke, wanting to be changed and fed. We sat in the rocker together while she ate, my foot gently pushing at the floor to keep us in motion. Rory finished feeding, and I raised her to my shoulder to burp her before heading back out to the kitchen. The baby was fed, but now my stomach was growling almost as loud as my bear.

For the next eighteen months, I raised my little cub, my Rory, as a single mom with help from the clan. Ian and Lauren were quick to include Rory with the twins. It was the cutest thing ever when Liam, Ian's younger son, would hold Rory's hand and walk with her around the small grassy area we had gated off for the little ones to play in when they were tired of being cooped up inside. It didn't matter the weather, these cubs loved to be out in the fresh air. And Trevor was always on hand whenever Rory needed anything too. Things only got better when Trevor met his mate, Rebecca. She is the sweetest, strongest person I had ever met. Well, next to Lauren.

Ian mated Lauren right after I broke things off with David. Soon after, the twins were on the way, and then my own little cub was born just a few weeks after that happy event.

"Heartbreak changes people..."

Chapter Four

David/Johnny

I wasn't the same man I had been. I had begun to fall deeper into the double life I was leading. I wasn't sure who the real me was anymore. I had a hair trigger temper, and some days, the depression was like a weight on my chest, suffocating me. That's what happens, you know. Heartbreak changes people, making them sad, mad, depressed, and sometimes, very self destructive. I was a changed man. We had returned to Fall City at Janet's orders. That psychotic bitch was out to kill the grizzly clan that had finally put an end to Hatchet's deadly, dangerous reign. She was hell-bent on destroying the one clan I wished she didn't know about. My Regan was a part of the clan that Janet was gunning after, and even though we hadn't been together in almost two years, she was still my heart, my soul. I should have listened when she asked me to leave Hatchet's crazy plans behind, but I was so caught up in the fact that I was a Secret Keeper on a very important mission that I was blinded to what was really the most important thing -- my fated mate, Regan. I missed her every day, but bit by bit, I was learning to live without her. Not living well, but I was alive, with a barely beating heart.

"David, come here," I heard Janet yell from the next room.

"Yo, what?" I answered back.

"Come here," Janet yelled again. "We have plans to make, and I have the perfect place for planning."

I walked into the other room where more of Janet's followers were sitting on various pieces of broken furniture. Most of them could do with a bath and a shave. The stench was overpowering and somewhat rancid. One of the men, Jeff, had food from last night's dinner still stuck in his unkempt scruffy beard, as if he was saving the crumbs for later.

Janet was standing by the door, holding court like a deranged queen watching over her equally deranged subjects. She looked over the gathering clan with a gleam in her eye, her madness shining through.

"Let's go to the bar," she said. "I feel like a drink."

We all filed outside to the waiting cars and climbed in, leaving the house. We pulled up outside of The

Roadhouse in Fall City and walked inside. As my eyes adjusted to the interior lights after being in the bright sun, we made our way to a back corner table and sat. I took the chair nearest the back wall so that I could scan the bar occasionally, watching for any signs of trouble. We had been sitting and listening to Janet spew her ideas of revenge for about twenty minutes when the door to the bar opened and one of the waitresses who had helped us before walked in, followed by Trevor Mannus, one of the bears from Marcus' clan. I reached out to stop Janet from going near him. That's just what we didn't need -- a shifter fight in the middle of a small town watering hole. Trevor's eyes followed the waitress. Rebecca, I thought her name might be. It wasn't something I paid attention to anymore really, women's names. I only had one woman's name on my mind and it didn't belong to a waitress, albeit a pretty one, but still her name wasn't at the top of my priority list.

Janet had been planning to rid the world of the Grizzly clan since Hatchet's death, and now that Trevor had a girlfriend, she was in danger too. This life was starting to wear on me. Janet outlined her plan to go after Trevor's new girlfriend, the waitress at the bar. She wanted him to suffer as much or more than she had when Hatchett had finally been taken out. Once she had Trevor neutralized, her plan was to take out Ian and his mate, Lauren, and finally, she was going after

Marcus. I had no love for him. I didn't even know him. My biggest concern was Regan and how she could be caught in the crossfire of this never ending war between the grizzlies and black bears.

After several more beers all around, Janet decided we should head back to the house and reqroup. We all stood, headed out the door, and got into our vehicles. As luck would have it, Janet ended up with me. Once on the road, I broached the subject again to see if I could change her mind.

"Janet, I think that we should give up on this plan of yours," I said.

"Give up? Give up?! No, absolutely not," Janet replied with a crazed look in her eye. "I won't give up until the grizzly clan is dust and ash under my feet."

"I just feel...," I tried again.

"No, David, the plan continues. Trevor's new toy is dead, Trevor is dead," Janet answered, "Ian and his bitch are dead, and then I will rip the meat from Marcus' bones myself."

I stopped trying to reason with her after that. I knew it wouldn't do any good. We arrived back at the house, and I stepped out of the car and headed inside. Inside my room, I sat on the edge of the bed and tried to decide the best way to stop Janet's plan. I knew I had to, at the very least, warn Rebecca and Trevor of the looming danger from Janet's insanity. I began to walk towards the front door when I was stopped by Jeff, the scruffy bearded member of our clan.

"Where're you going, pretty boy?" Jeff slurred, already drunk at 2 o'clock in the afternoon.

"I'm headed out to run some errands, Jeff," I replied.

Jeff stumbled to the left, so I went to the right and out the door to my truck. I got in, started the engine, and headed into Fall City to find Trevor and his girl.

I rolled my window down and let the wind blow into the cab of the truck. The wind brought me back to almost two years before...

Headed down the same road, Regan had her bare feet up on the dash, singing along to some twangy country song I'd never heard about kicking your ass, smiling and coasting her hand out her open window as we headed for our secret meeting place, the pond just down the road from their clan compound. We arrived at the little dirt road we would park on before heading back into the trees to the pond. Once there, we sat and held hands like teenagers, talking until the stars came out.

Just after twilight, Regan smiled up at me, tilted her head, and said, 'Babe, let's go swimming.' I laughed, thinking she was kidding, and said, 'Regan, we don't have suits.' She smiled even bigger and started to remove her shoes. 'Who needs clothes?' I watched as she got down to her panties and bra, then I watched as she made a run for the cool water of the pond.

I was mesmerized, entranced. She was the most beautiful thing I'd ever seen. Long red hair, green eyes and the hottest little smile. She looked like a water nymph and she was it for me. I knew eventually we would be together. I just needed to finish this mission entrenched in the clan with Hatchet. Then we could start our lives.

I stood up and toed off my boots. Stripping down to my skivvies and jumping in after her, I swam up to her and snagged her waist. Pulling her to me, I smiled and held her tight as I headed for deeper water. Her eyes lit up and her smile got even more mischievous than it already was. She leaned in and kissed me sweetly. I returned her kiss, taking it deeper, drawing a small moan from her throat as she levered herself closer to me. My hands tangled in her hair, taking control and feasting on her lips. I was a starving man, and she was my sustenance.

She pulled away from me. Raising one hand and wrapping it around my neck, she breathed in and said, 'I need you, David.' I hated when she called me that. I struggled with not wincing. My bear was close to the surface and not any happier about her calling me by my undercover identity when we were together intimately. But I knew I couldn't tell her the truth. She'd never understand.

I arrived at Rebecca's moms house almost three hours later. The drive was just what I needed to remember my Regan. Pulling into the driveway, I was pulled from my memories of my time with Regan. I parked in the driveway and walked up to the door. I stopped in front of it and knocked.

Rebecca's mom answered, "Yeah, what do you want?"

"Hi, I'm David," I answered. "May I come in, ma'am?"

"I suppose," she threw over her shoulder as she headed towards the kitchen.

I followed her in and closed the door. She sat at her dinette table, so I pulled out one of the other chairs to sit and I began,

"Ma'am, I'm here to warn you about a plan to hurt your daughter."

"You may as well call me Lisa," she said. "Now, who the hell wants to hurt her?"

"A very crazy lady, Lisa," I replied. "Her name is Janet, and she is planning to kill your daughter."

"Did Alan put you up to this?" she asked in disbelief.

"I don't know anyone named Alan," I answered. "I'm close to Janet and I don't want anyone to get hurt."

Lisa scoffed at me. I watched in amazement as she shook her head, not taking me seriously. This may have been a bad idea after all. I tried again to get her to listen to my concerns, but it was no use. She was convinced that it was a joke. As I was getting ready to leave, I heard the front door open and then I heard voices in the hall. One of the voices had to be Rebecca, but the other voice, I recognized. It was Trevor. Fuck, I thought.

I watched as Trevor headed into the kitchen at a fast pace, slamming into me. He took me down to the ground. I could hear Lisa yelling at him but I couldn't really make out her words as I saw Trevor's fist hurtling towards my nose. His fist slammed into my face, the sound of cracking cartilage resounding off the walls of the enclosed kitchen. He drew his fist back to strike another blow but he was taken out by a frying pan to the head and he went down hard. He didn't lose consciousness, but I was sure he was seeing stars. He reared back and let out a growl of frustration and pain. By this time, I'd managed to wiggle out from under his suffocating large frame and was sitting up holding my nose, the blood running in rivulets down my face and onto my t-shirt. I heard Rebecca come into the room, and we both turned to look at her. I waited to hear Trevor tell her to get out of the kitchen for her safety. But instead, I watched as she aimed a double-barrel shotgun at me, and then I heard I her ask,

"What the fuck is going on?" She seethed in anger. "Why are you guys beating each other up, and who the hell are you?" She pointed the gun directly at me and stared.

"My name is Johnny Wallace," I answered nasally. "I'm here trying to stop Janet and the rest of Hatchets clan from doing anymore damage."

"Johnny?" Trevor yelled. "Since when is your name Johnny, David?"

"It's always been Johnny," I answered. "I've been undercover for the last three years, trying to stop Hatchet and now Janet from exposing us to the world at large."

"Well, Johnny, you're too late," Trevor growled out. "There is already more damage done."

"What the hell are you doing in this house?" Rebecca yelled at me, interrupting Trevor.

"I'm here trying to warn your mother and you about what Janet has planned," I began.

"What the fuck is that psycho bitch planning?" Trevor asked in anger.

"She is waiting until Rebecca is alone at the bar to take her and use her to trade for you and Ian," I said, still holding my nose and speaking with a nasally tone. I grimaced at the pain I was in.

"And what about Regan?" Trevor asked me seriously.

"That's none of your business," I replied testily. "I'm just here to warn you guys to be vigilant in Rebecca's safety and then I'm gone."

"You can't leave. Regan needs you," Trevor yelled. "She and Rory are in the hospital."

"Rory, who the hell is Rory?" I asked bewildered.

"Rory is Regan's daughter," he answered.

"Daughter?" I asked distractedly, "When did she have a cub? I mean, a baby?"

"Almost two years ago," Trevor replied. "You didn't know? I know you two were close, so I thought you knew."

I closed my eyes in pain. I hadn't known that Regan was pregnant with my cub when we broke up. If I'd known, I never would have picked my mission over my family.

Trevor looked at me and said, "You can't just leave. You need to go and talk with her."

I opened my eyes and said on a sigh, "I know."

We all sat at the table, Lisa looking confused, Rebecca bouncing her knee in frustration, Trevor looking around and taking in the room, and me looking down at my clasped hands. I wasn't really paying attention, lost in my thoughts of Regan and my cub. I wondered why she hadn't told me. It was one of the questions I would need to ask when I finally caught up with her. I was so lost in thought that I almost missed when Trevor started to speak.

"Johnny, I need to know what the hell Janet is doing," Trevor said.

"She plans on taking out Marcus and all the others, including you. But definitely Ian. She hates him for killing Hatchet," I replied. "We're holed up in a house off of West River road. I think that some of the guys are getting ideas about why I'm there. Jeff especially watches me too closely."

"Alright, this is what we need to do," Trevor said as he began to outline a plan to stop Janet from hurting his mate or anyone else. "Johnny, you'll go back and act natural, but keep me informed if Janet's plans change."

"I will," I said as I got up to leave. "Trevor, where is Regan at right now?"

"She's in the hospital," Trevor replied. "There was an explosion at the compound. Janet and a few others were there including Jeff and James when they escaped, they blew the main meeting building sky high. Regan and Rory were caught in the blast."

I panicked, thinking only of getting to my injured mate. I asked in a worried tone, "Which hospital are they in?

"They're at Snoqualmie Valley, Room 212," Trevor answered me lightly.

"Thanks. I'll call if anything else comes up," I said and then headed to the front door.

"I only miss you when I'm breathing..."

Chapter Five

~ Regan ~

I watched the twins playing with Rory out in the small playground that we had put together, smiling at their antics. They were both so protective towards her, it always made my heart warm to see. Noah was always keeping his eyes on Liam and Rory both, as he was the 'older' brother. Seeing Rory everyday was bittersweet for me; she looks so much like David that every once in a while, I can't catch my breath from missing him so much. I'm still mad at him, don't get me wrong, but some days, I wished he was here to share in our lives. He is missing so much of Rory's first years, her first steps, her first words. Those times can't be relived. I wonder if I should just go out and find him to tell him about my little cub.

"Kids, let's go," I called out. "It's time for lunch."

The twins, Rory, and I all headed towards the cabins. Lauren opened the door to her home and called the boys in. I waved as we headed towards the main meeting building. We were making lunch today for the older members of the clan. Rory loved to sit at the table where we made sandwiches and other snacks for everyone who wanted to join us.

We entered the building and headed for the kitchen area at the back. Once we got to the fridges, I started to take the makings for ham and cheese sandwiches out. Setting everything on the table, I said to Rory,

"Well, little cub, are we ready to make lunch for everyone?"

'Yep, mama," was her enthusiastic reply.

I laughed at her energy and started putting the sandwiches together. The next thing I remember is waking up in the Snoqualmie Valley hospital hooked up to machines and wondering what the hell had happened.

"Where's Rory?" I asked the nurse checking my vitals.

"She's with your father," she kindly replied.

"Thank you," I said. "Could you get my dad for me, please?"

"Of course, I'll send him right in," she stated. "He's been very worried about you."

I watched the nurse leave the room to go and get my father. Once she was gone, I let the fear out. I couldn't remember what had happened but I was pretty banged up. I had a broken wrist and I could also feel a pretty big lump on my head. The door to my room swung open and there stood my dad, holding Rory and looking concerned, maybe a little scared.

"Regan, sweet pea, are you ok?" he asked me in a worried tone.

"I'll be fine, Daddy," I replied, reaching for my little cub to make sure she was ok. "Don't worry, the injuries are already starting to heal."

'Thank God," he whispered.

Rory cuddled into me. I held her close as my dad explained what had happened. Janet and the others had apparently planted a bomb in the main meeting building where I was putting lunch together, with the help of my little cub. When the explosion happened, we were trapped in the rubble. While Trevor and my dad were digging us out, Janet and the rest escaped. It was all a diversionary tactic to get away. We could have died.

They stayed with me for quite a while, both of us adults seeming to have a hard time with what could have been. My dad couldn't take his eyes off of me, and I couldn't let go of Rory.

"I'm gonna take Rory home," my dad said. "She's fine, but she definitely needs a nap."

I tightened my arms around Rory. I didn't want to let her go, but I knew my dad was right. If she didn't need to be here, then the best place for her was at home, surrounded by her own things and the rest of the clan. I reluctantly let my dad take her from my arms. With one last kiss on the check for my little cub and one from my dad, they left to go home.

I sat up in my hospital bed, still unsure what had happened. I think I was lucky I couldn't remember the bomb going off. Maybe it would save me on the nightmares.

I heard my door open slowly and turned to see who was coming through. My breath caught as I whispered out, "David…"

"Regan, are you ok?" the man who had left me asked.

"I will be," I replied. "What are you doing here?"

"Trevor told me you were here," he said. "I had to make sure you were alright."

"Why do you care?" I asked him sullenly, my heart breaking all over again at just seeing him standing here.

David walked up to my hospital bed and leaned over. Looking me in the eyes, he said,

"I never stopped caring."

I watched his eyes roam over my injuries, stopping to look at my wrist and then traveling up to see the bruising on my face. He made a noise at the back of his throat, a cross between a growl and a groan of pain. He slowly reached his hand towards my face to cup my cheek, but I moved away from him at the last minute. There were so many things we needed to discuss, Rory being the biggest. David had no idea that she even existed. How was I going to tell him that he had a little girl?

"Baby, you sure are banged up," he murmured.

"I'll be fine, thank you," I replied. "Please don't call me baby..." I was too beat up to be able to deal with his whispered endearments or the way his eyes were watching me.

"Regan, we need to talk," David started to say.

"I know we do," I interrupted. "But it can wait until I'm out of here."

Just as I finished speaking, the nurse walked back into the room.

"Miss Jensen, the doctor will be in shortly to let you know when you can go home," my nurse said as she looked at David, and I could feel my bear becoming agitated. No one was to look at my mate, unclaimed or not. I couldn't control the growl in my throat that was threatening to be released. Just as I thought my bear was going to win over my human side, I felt David take my hand in his and gently stroke my palm, calming my bear and my soul.

As the nurse left the room, I pulled my hand from David's light grip, trying to regain my balance. I knew we would eventually see each other, but not like this. Not when I was injured and hurting, my mind clouded by painkillers, wanting to fall into him and never let go. I watched him through lowered eyes, wondering what he was doing standing in the middle of my hospital room looking at me like he had never stopped loving me. I still loved him. He was my one, my Fated Mate. I raised my chin and looked him in the eye, asking,

"What do you want, David?"

"You, Regan. I want you," he responded.

"Well, I'm sorry," I answered. "I'm not available at the moment." I knew I was lying to David but I couldn't tell him about Rory yet, so maybe a small lie about not being free would give me some time to decide how to discuss his daughter with him.

I watched David, longing to be closer to him but knowing that if I told him about our little one, he would hate me forever.

"Regan," David began, "I have so many things to tell you, but I don't know where to start."

"We can't do this, David," I said. "I don't want you here. I needed you to be here two years ago but not now. Get out! Just go!.."

David stared at me for another long moment and then with a very long sigh, he said, "Alright, Regan, I'll go for now. But I'll be back later. We have to talk."

I watched as he headed for the door. Just before opening it to leave, he turned, looked at me, and said,

"I've loved you for a long time, Regan. Being away from you for the last eighteen months hasn't changed the way I feel. I can't breath for thinking of you."

Then he left, walked out the door just like I had ordered him to. I couldn't believe he didn't stay to fight it out like we had in the past when we had a disagreement. He just left. I watched the door for several minutes waiting for him to come back, waiting for him to decide that he wanted to fight for me, for us. He said he loved me as I laid here and said nothing of what was in my heart, in my soul. It was like my heart was breaking all over again. As I stared at the door, it was slowly pushed open. Hoping it was David, I sat up a little straighter. Once the door was pushed all the way open to reveal the doctor, I deflated, all the air going out of me on a broken exhale.

"Ms. Jensen, you are a very lucky woman. That explosion, by rights, should have done much more damage than what you have," he said as he checked my vitals and began to ask me inane questions about the date, who the President was, and my first name and age. They were the same questions that the nurse had asked me earlier, and my answers hadn't changed from then till now.

"When can I go home, Doctor?" I asked with hope in my voice.

"If you have no issues overnight, I should be able to discharge you tomorrow," he replied, smiling.

"Thank you. I can't wait to get home to my little girl," I said to him.

"Yes, your daughter is a cutie. I was the doctor on call when you were both brought in," he stated. "You protected her very well, Ms. Jensen."

"It's what a mom is supposed to do, Doctor," I said with a small smile as I thought of my little sunshine.

"Well, if you need anything, please use the call button for the nurse," the doctor said as he began to gather his things to go. "If you have any issues at all, I need to know right away, so don't be tough, Ms. Jensen."

"I won't. Thank you again, Doctor," I said as he left through the same door that David had walked out of nearly an hour before.

After the doctor and nurse left, I sat and thought back to the day my little cub was conceived. It was the day we went skinny dipping in our pond, one of my favorite memories of our time together. Until just a month later when, at that same amazing spot, we both made one of the hardest decisions of our lives. I knew David was keeping something from me. I could tell through our tenuous bond that had never been completed.

I laid my head back on the pillows and stared at the ceiling for what seemed like hours. The sound of the door opening yet again yanked me from my musings of what my life would have been like if David and I had mated when we first realized that we were meant to be. I glanced at the opened door to see Trevor standing there looking concerned and a little guilty.

"Hey, Bug," Trevor said. "How are you feeling?"

"I'm fine, Trevor," I replied. "Dad told me you pulled us out of the rubble. Thank you for that."

"I would do it all over again, Bug," Trevor said with emotion choking his words. "You're my sister. Why wouldn't I?"

"Trevor, I'm fine," I reiterated. "I get to come home tomorrow, the doctor said."

"I'm glad, Bug," he said. "I've got something to tell you though..."

"What is it?" I asked him with curiosity.

"I saw David today," he said. "I'm the one who told him you were here. I'm sorry, Bug. I should have seen what's been in my face this whole time."

I sat in silence for several minutes, and then Trevor began to talk again.

"I know he's Rory's dad, Regan."

I gasped and said, "How could you know that? No one knows who her father is."

"I saw you together before, remember?" Trevor reminded me gently of the day that I walked away from David. "I promised not say anything then but I had to say something now, Bug."

"Trevor, what the hell did you do?" I shouted at him in a panic.

"I told him about Rory. At the time, I hadn't put two and two together to get four," he answered me calmly, which caused my panic to rise even more.

"How could you?" I whispered, hurt evident in every word.

"I'm sorry, Regan," Trevor said, turning to go. "I'm really, really sorry."

As the door closed behind him, I thought to myself about why David hadn't said anything about my little cub, my Rory. I wondered if he was angry. He hadn't acted angry earlier, just sad. I had to talk to him before it was too late. I had to make this right, as soon as possible. Reaching down, I pressed the button to call the on duty nurse. She bustled in asking if I was in any pain. I answered her,

"No, no pain. Can you tell me where the man who was here just before the doctor went?"

"Well, he's outside in the waiting room, hon," she answered in surprise, acting as if I should know where he was.

"Could you get him for me please?" I asked quietly.

"Of course. I'll be back shortly with that nice young man," she said as she left the room. I took a deep cleansing breath, then another and another, knowing that I would have to have a deep discussion with David now instead of after I'd left the hospital.

The nurse came back with David in tow. I watched him walk over to the chair near the windows that overlooked the parking lot below. Sitting down, he leaned forward to rest his elbows on his knees. I looked into his beautiful green eyes, so like Rory's, and lost another little piece of my heart to him. It's been said that even a broken heart can love, and I guess that was the proof right there.

"Hey, baby," David started. "The nurse said you wanted to see me."

"David," I said, my voice cracking from the unshed tears that I was barely holding in. I took a shuddering breath before continuing, "I'm sorry, so sorry I didn't tell you earlier." I started to cry, unable to hold in the tears that had built up and spilled over.

David stood up and came to the side of the bed, sitting on the edge he gathered me up in his arms, holding me gently but firmly, running his hand through my hair and making shushing noises as I cried. The pain came out in each shuddering breath, with each fallen tear. I cried for the lost time, I cried for our daughter, I cried for David, and lastly, I cried for myself. It was a healing cry, one that had been long overdue.

"Baby, I need you to listen to me," David said. "You need to know that I am still with Hatchet's fractured clan, but not for the reasons you think."

I had finally stopped crying, my tears slowly stopping as I breathed a little raggedly, but I was able to say to David,

"Why, David? What is so important that you stay? Make me understand."

"Do you know what the Secret Keepers do?" he asked me.

"Ummm, I think so," I answered him evasively. "They keep our laws and sometimes have to pass judgement."

"That's right, baby," he said. "I've been a Secret Keeper for almost six years."

I gasped in surprise. This was one thing I had never considered, that he had been undercover with Hatchet and the rest. I was stunned. Speechless.

"Wait, I thought the Secret Keepers identity was never to be revealed," I asked, knowing full well that the oath was the one I had taken myself not even four years earlier.

"We aren't, but I couldn't keep lying to you," he said. "You should probably also know that my name isn't David. It's Johnny. I'm sorry I lied to you. It was part of my job. I wasn't allowed to tell anyone who I really am."

"I know, Johnny," I said, trying out his real name for the first time and liking how it felt rolling off my tongue. "I know because I have something to say to you, too."

"I already know about Rory, baby," he stated. "That isn't really a secret anymore."

"That's not the only secret I've been keeping," I told him. "I've been a Secret Keeper for four years."

He stared at me for long moments, then slowly he started to grin. His grin turned into a full blown smile in no time flat. Once his smile was lighting up almost his whole face, he began to laugh, a huge mirth filled sound. I worried he was in shock, he laughed for so long. Thinking I would need to snap him out of his hysteria, I was reaching up to give him an open-handed tap to the cheek when he stopped laughing. He looked down at me and said,

"You've got to be kidding me. Fate must be laughing her ass off right now."

"You're probably right, babe." I laughed a little in response, wondering if I should ask him what was next. Did he want to meet his daughter; did he want to continue on his mission; did he want to restart our relationship? I had so many questions but I was mentally and physically exhausted and could barely keep my eyes open. I yawned, trying to hide it behind my hand. Johnny caught me yawning though, and I was sure he would tell me to rest.

Instead, he said, "Baby, scootch over. I'm gonna hold you while we talk, okay?"

I moved over to give him more room. As he climbed into the too small bed and snuggled me close, I sighed contentedly, loving the feeling of safety and love I could feel radiating from him, joining with my soul and soothing the inner beast. My bear had been an angry bitch for the last eighteen months, missing our mate, pining for him. She would only be gentle with our cub. If I shifted and one of the guys of the clan came too close, she would react violently. So many times Trevor and Ian barely missed being cut to ribbons by my claws.

I rubbed my cheek on his forearm and cuddled into his large frame, leaching his warmth into my bones. I was always cold no matter how many layers I wore and lying in the hospital where they kept the temperature on frozen, I was appreciating the extra warmth.

"Which of us is going to go first?" I asked.

"Let me tell you a story first, ok, baby?" he said.

"The hurt comes in waves, and tonight I'm drowning..."

Chapter Six

David/Johnny

I pulled Regan's lush body against my larger frame, holding her tightly. I was afraid this was one of those too real dreams that you wake up from way too soon. I mulled over what I was going to say. I had already told her too much. As I relaxed next to her on the bed, I began the story of how I had become a Secret Keeper in the first place.

"I need to tell you some things about my past," I began. "There's a reason that I became a Secret Keeper and why I have been undercover for so long."

And so I told her of the first time I saw Hatchet and his crew of miscreants.

I was 13 years old. I had been sent to the store to get milk for my little sisters. We had run out earlier in the day, but dad wasn't feeling well now. Mama had to stay with the little ones, so I volunteered to go. I walked the four blocks to the local grocery store. I was there for maybe fifteen or twenty minutes. I ran into a friend and lost track of time. God, why did I lose track of time? I talked with my buddy for a bit then headed home.

As I walked around the last corner and started towards my house, I saw several men get into an older Chevy that was all black and really badass parked at the end of our driveway. They were running for the car, one yelled over his shoulder "Let's go Hatchet, this was a bad idea." They looked like they were in a hurry. I watched as they flew down the road at a high rate of speed.

I remember walking to the front of the house and going in, but then I don't remember much other than the blood everywhere. There was so much blood. I don't know why I can't remember anything else. The cops showed up and questioned me. Even they didn't know how I couldn't remember anything other than the crimson red on the floor, the walls, and even up on the ceiling.

My mama, my sisters, and my daddy were all slaughtered for no good reason. Daddy didn't have a lot of money. Most of the time we were living paycheck to paycheck, barely able to eat let alone have anything to steal. That's what the police thought had happened, that the group of men were there to steal from us. Because daddy was sick, he couldn't protect them, and mama was human.

The police asked me so many questions. All I could tell them at the time was that there was a group of men who ran from our house and got into an older black Chevy muscle car. That was it, nothing else. I am haunted by nightmares still of the looks on everyone's face at the house. It will stay with me forever.

She was going to be shattered to know that I wasn't finished with my mission. Janet and the others needed to be stopped before it was too late. I struggled with how to tell her for several minutes when she turned her head, looked up at me with a sad little smile and said,

"Just say it, Johnny. I don't like it, but I understand."

"Baby, I have to finish this. I can't just walk away," I said as I watched her face contort in pain. I knew that I would hurt again, but I had hoped to ease the ache for her. She was my light in the darkness that was in my soul. The waves of depression that had been drowning me slowly were receding and giving way to a lightness I hadn't felt in years, not since the day we were there by the pond not realizing that was going to be our last time together. But Fate can't be stopped or beaten. That controlling bitch always gets her way, and now here we were cuddled up together and getting ready to bear our deepest secrets to each other.

"I know it isn't what you want to hear," I began.

"I know that this is a mission. I just wish I was more important to you," Regan interrupted with a long suffering sigh.

"You deserve so much better than me," I said. "You both do."

Regan turned her head and looked out the window into the softly fading light, deep in thought. I wondered where her head was at and if she could wait for me. I wondered if I should even make her wait. She was my fated mate. I should want to be with her and only her. I shouldn't want to finish this mission from headquarters. The Secret Keepers had taken up enough of our lives, but I also knew if I didn't stop Janet, she would murder the whole grizzly clan, including Regan and our daughter, who I hadn't even met yet.

I softly kissed her forehead and tightened my arms around her before saying,

"Baby, I have to go."

Regan stared at me for several minutes. She stared for so long I began to worry.

"I know you do," she said, "but can you wait a few more minutes? I really need to …"

"What did you want to tell me?" I interrupted as I hugged her to me tighter.

"I have so many things to tell you," she answered. "I need you to understand what was going through my head at the time."

I listened as she explained how scared she was to disappoint her father, her clan, even herself. I felt ashamed when she talked about not telling me of the baby because of my connection to Hatchet's clan. I was proud when she talked of her status as a Secret Keeper and scared when she told me of her missions.

But most of all, I was lucky and I knew it. I was certain Fate had picked the right one for me when Regan spoke of her great love of her baby, our cub. She was an amazing mother, and no child would ever want for anything with Regan in her corner.

"Baby, I get why you didn't say anything," I said. "I wish things were different, but the Fates work in weird ways and we just seem to be along for the ride."

"I know you're right," Regan said. "We've missed so many things because of my stubborness."

We gazed into each other eyes for what seemed like hours, but it was just mere moments in time. I finally broke eye contact with her to lean in and softly kiss her forehead. I tightened my arms around her before saying,

"Baby, I have to go."

"I know you do, Johnny," she answered back.

I slowly extracted myself from the too small bed, leaned in, and kissed her cheek before turning and headed to the door. Once I reached the closed door, I turned and said,
"This won't be forever, babe. I promise."

I watched Regan for a few moments and then walked out into the hallway. Once the door closed behind me, I let out a deep sigh of regret. I knew she wouldn't wait forever, but I just needed her to wait long enough for me to stop the madness that was coming for her family and mine.

As I left the hospital, I knew of only one way of stopping Janet and I didn't think I would be strong enough to do it. I knew if I caught her in the act of revealing the truth of shifters, it would be a righteous ending, but if I killed her before she did something that was against our laws, I would be putting myself in the crosshairs of other Secret Keepers. I couldn't do that to Regan and Rory. I just couldn't see a way around the crazy ride that I was on at the moment. I got into my car and headed for the house, hoping that Janet would come to her senses but knowing she probably wouldn't.

I turned into the driveway and slowed my car to a crawl; the potholes were almost as deep as the ditches that ran along the sides of the rural road our house sat on. I had told Hatchet before that we needed to do some upkeep on this place, but it had only gotten worse in the last eighteen months. I pulled to a stop next to one of the trucks and headed for the front porch.

Once I reached the porch, I walked up to the door and opened it, looking around for Janet and wondering where she was. As my gaze rested on the couch in the living room, I could see James watching some bullshit reality show about keeping up with 19 kids and counting. I was not a fan of people putting their lives all out there for the world to see. James watched the shit like it was the gospel. He looked up when I walked by the couch and said,

"Dude, Janet is looking for you."

"Great. Where is she?" I asked.

"She's in the back, enjoying herself after escaping from those grizzlies earlier," he replied. "You missed a hell of a fireworks show man."

"So I heard," I muttered as I walked towards the back of the house. Down the hallway and off to the left, Janet had left her door ajar, so I tapped on it before pushing it open the rest of the way. That was a mistake.

She was standing there with one of the guys, Jeff, between her legs, and was he ever going to town. It looked messy and a little painful for them both. I turned to walk out when Janet told me to stop. I stopped in the doorway, but I didn't turn back to look at her. This was not something I wanted to see. While she was beautiful on the outside, the poison that she had on the inside made her ugly.

"Where have you been, David?" Janet asked while pushing Jeff away from her. Looking over my shoulder, I saw her grab her robe and wrap herself in it. "You could always join us, David. I know you like what you see when you look at me."

It's difficult to hold my tongue and tell her exactly what I think of her and her men. Instead I say,

"I don't share, Janet. I never have and I never will."

She stuck her lower lip out in a pout and said, "That's always your answer."

"Sorry, James said you were looking for me," I stated. "What's up?"

"Where were you when we hit the grizzly compound earlier today?" she asked, with a suspicious gleam in her eyes.

"Running errands in town, like you told me to," I answered.

"Oh, yes, that's right," she said. "I just assumed you'd be done with those few things much quicker, David."

"Sorry, won't happen again," I said as I tried to diffuse the anger I could see rising in her eyes, "What are we doing next? I'm ready when you are."

"Next we hit them at night," she smiled wickedly, "while they all sleep securely in their beds."

"Good plan, Janet," I lied. "When do we do it?"

"Soon, David, very soon," was her answer.

I walked away from Janet and the guy who was still on his knees, waiting for the words from her to start feasting again. While I wasn't a prude, I also wasn't into voyeurism.

I went to my room and sat on the edge of my bed. I started to think, really think about what this mission was doing to me, to Regan, and to our baby. I had missed so much of her growing up, would she take to me when I was finally able to stop Janet and the others or would she see me as a stranger? I didn't need to ask that question out loud. My loyalty to the Secret Keepers had already cost me two years with my girls. I couldn't let it cost me anymore time. Once this mission was done, I was out for good.

"The heart wants what the heart wants..."

Chapter Seven

Regan

I laid on my hospital bed thinking of Johnny, hoping he'd make the right choice. I was still so angry, with him, with myself, with the way things had turned out. We should have been together for the last two years, not trying to get over each other. I hadn't had time to dwell on the heartache, except in the quiet hours of the night when Rory was asleep or out with Lauren, Ian, and their boys. I sometimes would lay awake and wonder if I could find David... Errr... Johnny. To tell him about our little cub, to claim my mate, and to have our happily ever after, but I also knew that I couldn't force him to make that choice. He'd have to do it on his own. I fell asleep thinking of his entrancing green eyes and the way he could make me feel with just a look: loved, cherished, and adored. I wanted him in my life, but even with him being undercover, I couldn't let him in. Not until Janet and the rest were gone, either in prison or dead.

Hours later, I heard the door open to my room. Opening my eyes, I could see William, one of the members of our clan who'd been asking me out for several months. Even though we weren't mates, he still was trying to get my attention. I think it had more to do with who my dad is than with any burning desire to be with me personally.

"Hello, William," I said as he walked up to the chair next to my bed. Sitting down he looked at me a little closer, saying

"Regan, shit, you look awful. Are you okay?"

"Thank you, William, for noticing," I answered. "I'm going to be fine. Thanks for asking."

"I didn't mean anything by it, Regan," he sputtered. "It just looks like it hurts is all."

"It does a little, William, and I know that isn't how you meant it," I said. "What are you doing here?"

Before he could answer, the door to my room opened again to reveal Johnny, looking just as handsome and dangerous as he had the day before. I was so screwed. I looked up into his eyes and could see every emotion -- love, jealousy, and even a small amount of contempt. Probably because William was so close to me on the hospital bed where I lay.

"What the hell is going on here?" Johnny asked angrily.

"Nothing is going on," I answered. "This is William, one of my clan mates. William this is David, an old friend."

William moved closer to the bed, reaching for my hand. I pulled away slightly, not really sure what the hell was happening. I looked at William and then at Johnny, wondering why there was a pissing contest going on in my hospital room. William was watching Johnny with suspicion, while Johnny was watching William with anger. If it wasn't happening to me, it would be really comical. I really needed them both to quit the macho bullshit. I was starting to get another headache.

"William, nice to meet you," Johnny said as he moved forward to shake hands with William. William reached out to do the same, wincing a bit when Johnny started to squeeze his hand in his large grip.

"David, you look familiar. Have you lived in Fall City long?" William asked while eyeballing Johnny.

"I just recently returned to town," Johnny said smugly.

"Ok, you two, I've had enough of the bullcrap. William, I am going home tomorrow, and we'll talk then," I said. "David, we can talk once William leaves."

William stood, leaned over the side of my bed, and placed a chaste kiss on my cheek. I could hear Johnny's rumbling bear the whole time. I told William good-bye and watched as he left. I would worry about talking with him later. This was too important a talk at the moment.

"Johnny, what are you doing back here?" I asked him. "I thought we talked already. You aren't ready to leave that fucked up clan, and I can't leave my clan either."

"I know what I have to do now babe," he answered. "I have to stop Janet once and for all."

"And how are you going to do that, Johnny?" I asked. "She hasn't committed a single death sentence crime; we've checked."

Johnny looked at me and raised one eyebrow. Cocking his hip, he leaned into the side of the bed I was on and then stopped a hair's breadth away from me, looking deep into my eyes, he said,

"Baby, I can't be with you while she is still alive. I have to get rid of her for good."

I trembled a little in reaction to his deadly serious tone. I knew he wasn't joking. This was a side to him I had never seen -- deadly, focused, and like he meant business. I didn't know what to make of his words.

"Johnny, you can't kill her if she hasn't broken any of our laws," I tried again. "She skates along the edges. This is the most serious thing she has done ever. Blowing up our main meeting area, I mean."

"I know, but there has to be something I can do," he said, the frustration evident in his voice.

"There probably is, but we need to talk more than you need to solve the problem of Janet," I said to him gently.

He sighed, looking at me with defeat. Knowing I was right didn't make me as happy as I thought it would; it made me a little sad. Johnny watched me for several minutes, sighing as he said,

"I love you, but my job is important too."

"I've lost someone who should have been the most important person in my world..."

Chapter Eight

Johnny

I watched Regan for several more minutes. I knew that I was wrong. I knew that I needed to put my family first. But sometimes it's hard to stop when you have had a single goal for such a long time. I needed to get my head out of my ass and man the fuck up. Soon, or I would lose Regan and my daughter all over again.

"Baby, I'm sorry I haven't put you first," I said. "It's hard to change mindsets in the middle of a task. But I can put you first."

"I know you can," she replied, "but you won't if you don't change your priorities."

"I know, babe. I'm working on it," I said. "I need to know what you want me to do."

"I want you to want to do the right thing for me and Rory, Johnny," she said. "That's what I want you to do."

"I need to know why you didn't tell me you were pregnant, Regan," I finally said, bringing to light the elephant in the room.

"I couldn't make you stay just because we were having a baby," she replied with tears choking her voice. "I needed you want to stay for me, not because it was an obligation."

"I wouldn't have thought you were an obligation. I have loved you for as long as I've known you were my mate," I said. "But I also had a mission to stop Hatchet and his clan."

"I knew that you were dedicated and that's why I didn't tell you," she said as the tears finally broke through. The rivulets that were tracking down her cheeks broke me. I couldn't keep this up... I needed to make a choice. I just hoped it was the right choice. I caressed her cheek, wiping the tears away.

"I think I know what I have to do, babe," I told her quietly. "I'll be back soon."

I leaned in and kissed her cheek, running my hand through her beautiful red hair.

"You better be," she replied.

"Love you, babe," I said as I turned and walked to the door.

"Johnny," she called out.

I stopped and turned around, searching her eyes.

"I love you too," she whispered.

I pivoted and opened the door.Walking through to the hallway, I saw the nurse from the day before. I gave a slight wave and headed towards the elevator. Hitting the ground floor button, I waited for the elevator to descend while thinking of the choice I was about to make, hoping that Janet wouldn't lose her shit and knowing that hope was in vain.

I got to my car and opened the driver's side door. Getting into the car, I started the engine and headed out of the parking garage. At the exit to the parking structure, I turned left and headed back to town and the house that we were staying at while Janet contemplated her revenge.

As I drove, I thought back to when I knew Regan was mine. *I had been in the local bar of The*

Roadhouse, nursing a glass of Fireball over ice when she and her clan mates came in to let off some steam. I looked up as the door to bar opened inward, and the light caught her fire red hair, making me catch my breath. I watched as she walked to the bar and ordered herself a drink. Her two friends that she was with were a couple of guys I knew who were like family to the Grizzly Clan princess. I knew who she was. I had never seen her before of course, but Hatchet had complained enough about the 'spoiled' princess of Marcus' that I would know her anywhere. I knew instantly like a punch to the gut that she was the one that the Fates had picked just for me. Of course, I couldn't act on it in that moment. I was surrounded by Hatchet's goons. Fuck, I was one of them. Sort of. But not really. I had been undercover with them for six months now, trying to get more information on their illegal activities. For some reason, Hatchet had a grudge on Marcus like no one's business. I knew I would have to find a way to get her attention. I just didn't have a clue as to how to do so without drawing the wrong scrutiny from the others.

I watched as she turned her head and laughed at something that Trevor said, a full bodied sexy sound that I wanted to cause on a daily basis. I was fucked.

"Betrayal is the only truth that sticks."

— Arthur Miller

Chapter Nine

Lisa/Jeff

Jeff watched as a car came barreling up the drive. He didn't know who it was, nor did he really care. He had just watched Janet, the woman he loved, die at the hands of that asshat Trevor and his equally disgusting mate Rebecca, a human waste of space. As the car got closer, he could see a woman with a brassy head of hair and a smirk on her face. He still wasn't sure who she was or what she wanted but he was ready for a fight.

The car stopped just at the steps to the porch where Jeff was leaning on the railing watching the day go by. Out stepped the trashiest woman he had ever seen. Not only did she have brassy hair, but her makeup was hooker thick on her lined faced. This one had seen better days.

"What do you want, bitch?" Jeff asked with contempt in his words.

"I heard most of your friends are dead," the woman replied. "Do you want revenge for the killings?"

"Who the fuck are you?" Jeff demanded.

"I'm Lisa, Rebecca's mother," she replied with anger. "I overheard a conversation that you need to know about and I'm here to help you."

"Help me? Bitch, you aren't going to help me," he said. "Let me give you some advice -- leave while you can. I can be very deadly."

"Let me say what I came to, and I'll leave," she said without fear.

"Whatever. Spill," Jeff said.

"I know why you were outnumbered," she began. "It all started when a stranger showed up at my house a few days ago."

She went on to tell him of David's visit from several days before, how he met with Trevor and told him that his name wasn't David and that he was undercover. How he was there to warn them all of the upcoming threat. How when he left the house, he was headed for the hospital and a woman named Regan. She also told him of the child that was hidden among the small group that lived in the compound, not realizing she was signing her own death sentence for her betrayal, the betrayal not only of her daughter, but of the clan itself.

"What the fuck?" Jeff yelled loudly, tightening his hands on the banister of the porch rail, his knuckles turning the palest white.

Jeff's mind was in turmoil. While he hadn't exactly liked David, he didn't think he was a traitor or a spy, someone not to be trusted. David had been with Hatchet's clan longer than even Janet. How could this have happened? How did no one know? What did he do now? Janet was gone, killed by Trevor during their raid on the grizzly clan compound. Jeff was inconsolable.

Janet was what he'd wanted all this time. She wasn't his mate, but she let him do things to her that made his head spin and his heart race, and the sex was always dirty, always rough. It was just what his bear needed on more than one occasion. Now she was gone forever because of Trevor and his little bitch, and apparently David was the one to tell all their secrets.

David needed to be ended. Period. What to do with the information the sleazy woman was sharing with him? He knew what he wanted to do. Kill David and the rest of the Grizzly clan that had taken away Janet. He just needed to figure out the best way to do it. He had just the way to get his revenge on the human who had mated with that idiot Trevor. Now to figure out what to do with David.

"So, is my information good?" Lisa asked.

"Maybe, maybe not," Jeff replied. "I'll have to see when and if David ever shows his face."

Lisa stood for a moment, remembering seeing Trevor and Rebecca from the woods only hours before. Rebecca's happiness should have made her happy but because of her utter selfishness, it only made her angry and bitter at her own child, a child she never really wanted. Rebecca's father insisted that she be born, and then he left when he'd had enough. Enough of her, enough of the constant yelling and screaming, just enough of everything.

Lisa needed to be the most important person in his eyes, and after Rebecca was born, that just wasn't the case. He left her emotionally bleeding, telling her she was too high strung and needed help. She needed help alright, but the one person who could've eased the pain left. She needed to make sure that Rebecca paid for making her father leave; if only the little bitch had never been born he would have stayed. Instead, Lisa was trapped with a child she couldn't relate to and trapped in a cycle of booze and men who never treated her right. This was the way she would finally get her revenge, her reward for putting up with Rebecca and her constant knowing stares.

"Well, let me know if my information is worthwhile," Lisa said as she turned to leave the porch.

"Wait," Jeff yelled after Lisa. "Where are you going?"

"I did what I came to do. It's time for me to go," she replied.

"Well, don't go yet. How about a drink?" Jeff said, his voice oozing charm.

Lisa looked Jeff up and down. While he didn't seem to bathe regularly, he was handsome in a hot, homeless guy way. It couldn't hurt to have one or two drinks with him. Lisa turned back to the house and made her way up the front steps. Stopping in front of Jeff, she smiled and said,

"Sure, I'll take a drink."

Jeff smiled at Lisa and held the door open, ushering her inside. He let the screen door slam shut behind them, and Lisa startled at the loud noise, giving a little high-pitched giggle.

Walking into the kitchen, Jeff stopped at the island littered with empty beer cans and half smoked cigarettes. The place was a disaster area, but nothing that really bothered Lisa. Rebecca usually cleaned up their house, so Lisa was used to living in a cluttered place now that her ungrateful daughter had abandoned her. Jeff turned to the fridge and opened the door, casting an eerie light across the dimly lit kitchen.

Pulling two bottles of Rainer beer from the shelf and popping the cap off of both of them, he handed one to Lisa. With a half hearted clink of the necks of the bottles, he smiled again and took a long draw of his beer. Lisa copied the gesture in a silent air toast of her own before guzzling down half the bottle. With a loud satisfied sigh, she pulled the bottle from her lips and swiped her tongue over the residue left over from her drink. Jeff watched as her tongue slid over first her top lip and then back again and over her bottom lip. Watching her through half slitted eyes, he took another pull on his beer, finishing the bottle in one last large gulp.

Putting the empty down with the rest of the half full bottles, he advanced on Lisa. He liked how her eyes got a little wider, her heart sped up a notch, and her cheeks reddened in lust. Jeff grabbed Lisa by the wrist in a crushing grip. Pulling her roughly against his body, he bent her back until she moaned in pain.

"Is this what you want, bitch?" he demanded in a primal growl. "To be used and discarded?"

With a moan of pleasure, Lisa said, "Yes, I like it a little rough."

"You might not like this," Jeff replied as he dragged her down the hall towards his room. Kicking the door open, he manipulated her body to the side of his bed. Pushing her down, he ripped her leggings down and off, leaving one leg of her pants hanging off her foot, exposing her pantyless ass. As Lisa struggled to move away from his groping hands, he took one large meaty mitt and whacked her asscheek with a resounding smack. Once her left cheek settled, he did the same to the right, causing Lisa to squeal in shock and pain.

"I told you that you might not like this," Jeff sneered, lewdly making Lisa spread her legs, exposing even more of her ass and her engorged wet pussy. Still struggling, Lisa began to softly cry, trying to move away from Jeff's punishing strikes. Now that her legs were spread, every third hit was landing on her gaping vag, the sting nothing like the light smacks she usually got from her lovers. Jeff was slapping her hard enough that Lisa could feel the reddening of each spot where his hands landed. With one last slap, Jeff unbuttoned his jeans while holding Lisa down at the small of her back, giving her just enough room to wiggle but not enough to get away. Lisa was still fighting to get away when Jeff slammed his dick up her ass, causing her to scream out. This was one of

Janet's favorite things to do and it was always tighter than any pussy he'd ever dipped his wick in. He loved the fight and the struggle; it always made him cum faster. As he rammed her again and again, Lisa started to hump back into his cock.

"Play with yourself, slut," Jeff ordered on a growl.

Lisa was finally getting into the roughness of the pounding that Jeff was giving her, so she slid one hand down to her clit and started to roughly finger herself while Jeff rammed her ass again and again. On a moaning hiss, she felt her cunt tighten and then a gush of her juices released and ran down her legs and onto her fingers. Jeff slammed into her one last time and came with a loud groaning yell. Slumping over her back, he let himself take a deep cleansing breath and then another. Pulling from her ravaged ass, he gave her a slap and turned her to her back. Pushing her up the bed, he straddled her waist and moved her hair from her face to say,

"I'm not done with you yet, cunt."

On a shaky breath, Lisa looked up into Jeff's crazed eyes and knew that he wasn't anywhere near done, even though he had dumped one load in her ass. His cock was still erect and ready for business. Moving slightly, she tried to get out from under Jeff, saying,

"I don't think I can go again. You surprised me what with ramming that big thing in my ass."

"That was my plan, bitch. Now shut up and take it," Jeff replied.

Jeff moved down her body and twisted one nipple with his fingers as his eyes traveled down her body. For an older bitch, her tits were still pretty perky and she had a flat stomach, although she looked like a two dollar hooker with her makeup running down her cheeks, her shirt rucked up under her pits, and her pants hanging off one leg from where they had gotten caught in his hurry to bury his cock in her tight ass. Now that he could take his time, he decided to play even rougher. Jeff took her other nipple between his fingers and pulled it away from her fleshy tit, twisting at the same time, causing Lisa to cry out in pain. He let her nipple bounce back to her chest and did the same thing to the other until she cried out again. Jeff did this two more times on each nipple. He then took Lisa's right nipple between his teeth and bit down, hard. Hard enough to make her whimper and struggle to get her tit out of his mouth.

Pulling away, he glared down into her eyes and lifted his free hand, slapping her cheek. Stunned, Lisa went limp. No more struggle, she lay there immobile and let Jeff do what he wanted to her.

Once Jeff was satisfied that she wouldn't struggle anymore in this position, he wrenched her legs open and shoved himself into her open hole. The slapping sounds of his balls hitting her ass as he bottomed out was the only noise in the room besides his growling moans. He watched as his cock disappeared into the abyss of her cunt, the wet sloppy noises making him harder than ever. He looked up into her blank eyes and decided to have even more fun. Taking both of his hands and wrapping them around her throat, he squeezed, enjoying when Lisa started to struggle again. This, this made him feel alive. The smell of her cunt and her fear enough to make him almost reach his peak a second time.

With a little more pressure, Lisa started to gasp and claw at his hands trying to get Jeff to loosen his hold. The world was hazy from the lack of oxygen. Jeff released his grip, allowing Lisa to pull in a lung full of air. She tried again to wiggle away, but when Jeff realized that she was moving again, he tightened his hands and squeezed even more tightly. Lisa struggled as Jeff choked her and pumped into her overused pussy. The room started to go black before Lisa's eyes. As she lost consciousness, Jeff tightened his hold even more, gave two more hard deep thrust and came, emptying his balls deep into the now dead woman.

The woman only wanted revenge on her daughter and instead, Lisa was fucked hard and murdered in a way that was poetic justice for a woman who had always put men above all else, including her child's happiness. All Jeff wanted was a shell to get off into, and then to eliminate any further complications, he murdered Lisa in a sex game gone horribly wrong.

Jeff pulled himself from her sticky cunt and pushed her body to the floor. Heading to the bathroom, he got into the shower to wash away the remnants of his release.

Once done, he dressed and headed back out the porch to wait and see if David had the guts to show his traitorous face.

"I regret the day I let you go..."

Chapter Ten

Johnny

Johnny got closer to the turn off for the house and was still thinking of Regan and how they would be able to make a life for themselves. He knew he needed to tell Janet he was done and that she was being taken in for questioning on the explosion and attacks on Trevor and Rebecca just before.

Johnny pulled his car to a stop and put it in park. Looking toward the porch, he could see Jeff standing on the porch looking angry, which wasn't an uncommon occurrence. Opening the driver's door, he stepped from the car and shut the door to head for the front door. Jeff stood from his slouched position on the railing, coming to his full height of 5'10" and puffing his chest up like a bird challenging another for breeding rights. This was no mating dance though. Jeff looked ready for a major fight, and Johnny had no clue what the idiot was mad about this time.

"Hey, Jeff. What's up, man?" Johnny asked as he got to the steps, looking up at the very angry man standing there.

"What's up?" Jeff yelled. "What's up? I don't know, man! What's up with you?"

"Where's Janet?" Johnny asked, looking around and noticing that the cars and trucks that usually took up space were nowhere to be seen.

"David, that's a good question, man," Jeff said as he advanced on Johnny, his fists clenching at his sides.

Before anything else could be said, Jeff shifted into his black bear, slamming into Johnny before he could shift to protect himself. Jeff hit him and they both went to the ground. Johnny's grizzly burst forth and swatted at Jeff's head, missing by a fraction of an inch. Jeff came at Johnny's throat, and to stop him, Johnny dodged to the right and lunged, hitting Jeff in the mid-section and flipping him sideways. Jeff staggered once and then righted himself on his paws. With an angry roar, Jeff charged again, hitting Johnny hard. They both rolled, throwing dust up as they fought. Johnny bit into Jeff's shoulder and with a jerking twist, pulled a large chunk of flesh from him. Jeff's fur was starting to matte with the flowing blood, but he staggered again and charged.

Johnny stood his ground and roared a challenge. Jeff answered with a bellow and, using what little strength he had, tried to hit Johnny again. But Johnny was ready for him and dodged his blow. On the return, he slammed him to the ground with his front paws and roared a warning just inches from his face. Jeff struggled to get up and away, to attack again. This is what he had to do; he had to avenge Janet.

Johnny roared again, knowing this wouldn't be over until he had ended this fight the only way he could. Jeff was going to have to die here in the yard.

Johnny opened his maw and snapped his jaws shut on Jeff's exposed throat. Breaking bone could be heard in the yard. Johnny could feel Jeff's windpipe collapsing. With one last shuddering breath, Jeff was finally still. No breathing, no movement. Just dead.

Jeff shifted back to his human form upon his last breath, cuts and bruises covering his body. Some of the bruising was definitely from a previous fight.

Johnny moved away from the body and shifted back to his human self. Moving gingerly to the front door, he headed to his room to gather his things before Janet returned to see her favorite pet dead in the front yard.

At his door, he stopped and listened. Hearing no one else, he entered his room grabbed his clothes and dressed in a hurry. He needed to get back to the hospital and back to Regan. She was to be released soon, within the next day or so, and Johnny couldn't wait to finally meet his baby girl, his cub.

Once he was done gathering his meager belongings, he headed for the back of the house where some of his things were kept in a back bedroom. Moving along the hall, he noticed that Jeff's door was open.

Glancing in as he passed, he stopped, backed up, and looked again. On the bed was the body of an overused woman. He moved to the bed and looking closer, he could see that the woman was Rebecca's mother, Lisa. He didn't know what had happened, but he knew he would have to tell Rebecca that her mother was gone.

Shaking his head, he left the room and headed to his car. Spinning the wheels and throwing gravel, he left his undercover life behind. If Janet wanted to come after him, that was her choice. He would be ready; he would protect his family at all costs.

Now it was time to claim his mate, like he should have from the very beginning. Forget Janet, forget Hatchet's leftover rejects. His time as a Secret

Keeper was coming to an end. His family was his number one priority.

He raced down the road towards the hospital, not wanting to wait to tell Regan that he was finally free, that he was ready and he now knew that the most important thing in his world was her and their baby.

"Am I really your choice or just the consolation prize?"

Chapter Eleven

Regan

I had been doing a lot thinking since Johnny had left my room, two hours' worth of thinking. I knew that I wanted to be with Johnny, but I was still so angry at him for not choosing me in the first place. My anger was misplaced, and I knew it was. I was being unreasonable. But I had been so hurt two years before when he hadn't chosen me that I had felt my feelings were justified. Now I wasn't so sure. I still had to protect my little cub. Rory was still the most important part of my life, but her father was starting to become important to me again.

As I sat contemplating the what ifs and the whys, the door opened to reveal Trevor standing there looking grim. He entered the room and sat in the chair next to the hospital bed. Looking at his clenched hands, I knew he had something important to tell me -- bad but important.

"Ree, I need to tell you something," he began. "Janet won't be a problem anymore."

"What do you mean?" I asked him, unsure of what was going on. Being here and away from the clan was like being banished, so I had no clue what had happened for the last several days.

"Janet and several of the others showed up early this morning. She snuck into my cabin and tried to kill Rebecca and me," Trevor said. "I had to defend myself and my mate. Janet, and everyone that was with her, is dead."

I stared at Trevor for several moments, trying to process what he was saying and wondering if Johnny knew about this newest development. As I sat thinking, I could see Trevor shift uncomfortably in the too small chair, trying to keep his large frame from falling from the seat.

"So, what does this mean for the clan?" I asked nervously.

"For the clan? Not a lot. She attacked us. The kill was justified," Trevor replied. "But for you, it could mean everything."

I heard what Trevor was trying to say. On one hand, I was glad that the fight was finally over with Janet and the rest of Hatchet's psycho clan. But I also worried that now Johnny didn't have to make a choice and that just like when I found out I was pregnant, he would be trapped. While I was stuck in my head, I heard Trevor stand up and tell someone hello. Looking towards the door, I saw Johnny looking disheveled but still one of the hottest men I'd ever seen. Smiling up into his eyes, I said,

"Hey, babe. I missed you."

"You too, love," Johnny replied, smiling slightly and heading towards me. He gave Trevor a chin lift in greeting and then bent at the waist and took my face between his hands before capturing my lips in a sweet, soft kiss.

Wrapping my arms around his neck, I deepened the kiss, trying to get closer to his warmth. Being in the hospital was like being in a walk-in cooler all the time. They didn't seem to believe in heaters. And two thin ass blankets just weren't cutting it. Johnny's left hand went to the back of my head. Threading his fingers through my hair, he maneuvered me into a better position to take our kiss even deeper, slowly swiping his tongue into my mouth where we tussled for dominance. I heard Trevor loudly clear his throat to get our attention. Giggling, I pulled back and looked at Trevor. Johnny groaned softly at the back of his throat, which caused my giggle to become a full-blown laugh.

"Man, must you do that in front of me?" Trevor asked in slight disgust.

"Well, yeah," Johnny replied on a husky laugh. Grabbing my hand, he sat on the edge of the bed and draped his other arm around my shoulders, pulling me closer and hugging me to his side.

"Johnny, I have something to tell you," Trevor started to say. I could feel dread rising in me, knowing what he was about to say and hoping that Johnny didn't feel as if he had been cheated out of finishing his mission.

"I have to say something to Regan first, if that's ok?" Johnny said. "Regan, sweetheart. I'm done with the mission. I left Janet's hodge podge of bears. I chose you, you and Rory."

"Why? How did you decide?" I asked him in confusion. Did he already know about Janet?

"I was driving back to the house and I knew that I needed to be just with you and Rory. I mean, I still haven't even met my daughter yet... And I was worried about Janet and my mission. Now I see exactly what I need to do," Johnny explained. "I need to be with my family."

"I have waited two years to hear those words from you, but you need to listen to Trevor," I said.

"What's up, man?" Johnny asked Trevor.

"Janet's dead, Johnny," Trevor said without preamble. "She and several others attacked us as we were sleeping early this morning. I didn't have any other choice."

"Well, of course you didn't," Johnny replied. "I would have done the same if she'd come for my mate and my family."

"I know you would," Trevor said.

"Trevor, I have to tell you something as well," Johnny said. "I found Lisa at the house when I went for my things."

"What was she doing there?" Trevor asked.

"I don't really know. Jeff was there too," Johnny said. "That's why I look like this. We fought. But you need to know, I think she was there to start trouble."

"I wouldn't put it past her," Trevor replied. "I'll talk to her the next time we go to visit the house."

"Yeah, that isn't going to work," Johnny said. "I found her at the house, but she was dead."

"Dead? What? How?" Trevor sputtered. "What the hell am I going to tell Rebecca?"

"Calm down. It didn't look like she suffered," Johnny lied, hoping to spare Trevor from having to tell Rebecca the grisly details of what he'd seen. "I know that's no consolation."

Trevor stared at Johnny for several seconds, still in disbelief. Then he turned for the door and left without a backward glance. His thoughts in turmoil, he left the hospital and went to find Rebecca.

Johnny watched Trevor leave. He felt bad about the way he had blurted out the news. But what else could he have said? Lisa was dead.

"Baby, don't worry about Trevor," I said. "My dad is on his way here with Rory."

"I'm ready to meet my girl," Johnny said through the emotions clogging his throat.

"I figured you would be," I said. "I get to finally go home today as well."

"That's great news!" Johnny said. "Why didn't you say so before?"

"I was waiting for Trevor to leave," I said. "Plus I wanted you to be prepared for my dad's arrival."

I started to laugh, knowing that Johnny was quietly freaking out on the inside about my dad coming and bringing our little cub.

"Sorry doesn't mean anything unless you mean it..."

Chapter Twelve

Johnny

I watched Regan smiling at me as I was slowly going nuts inside my head. What the hell was I going to say to her dad? Better yet, what was I going to say to the daughter that I didn't even know?

"Baby, what do we need to do to get you ready to blow this joint?" I asked Regan. I knew if I kept busy, my freak out would stay in the background of my thinking.

"I need to put on my own clothes, which my dad is bringing with him," she replied. "I also need a shower, but a nurse is supposed to be back soon to help with that."

I wiggled my eyebrows at her, laughing I said, "Babe, I can help you with a shower."

Just as I finished my sentence, a loud voice behind me said,

"I don't think so, young man."

Oh shit. Regan's dad had arrived as I was openly flirting with her, just my luck. Rolling my eyes skyward, I sent up a prayer and turned to introduce myself to the man who had raised my mate. But before I could say hello, my eyes fell on the absolutely perfect little girl at his side. She was the image of her mother, except she had my eyes and hair color with just a touch of red, making it an amazing strawberry blond. I was in awe of this little girl that we had created. I had missed too much already and in that moment, I knew I would never miss another moment, no matter what happened.

Falling to my knees I just looked at Rory, not sure what to say or do. I watched her little hand drop from her grandfather's and one finger of her opposite hand went to her mouth, probably a comforting measure on her part. She looked back at me, then looking up at her grandfather, she watched as he gestured for her to come forward. She walked towards me. At the last minute, she changed her mind though and headed straight for Regan. Jumping up on the bed next to her mom, she started talking nonsense words about a million miles a minute.

"Son, let's go outside while these two talk. Rory's missed her mom," Marcus said to me. I looked up at him and got up off the floor. Marcus -- one, Johnny -- zero.

I followed Marcus out into the hallway, we let the door close to keep Rory in the room in case she decided to follow her Grandpa Marcus. We stopped a few doors down from Regan's room. I leaned against the wall and waited to see what Marcus was going to say.

"Boy, you have a lot to make up for," Marcus began. "What the hell were you thinking, getting my little girl pregnant and then leaving her? You didn't even claim her. No bullshit, either. I know you're her mate. She wouldn't have decided to be with you if you weren't."

I let his words sink in. I wasn't about to tell him that his sweet innocent little girl wasn't pure. Not that there was anything wrong with her having experience. Not even close. It made our sex life so much hotter. But he definitely didn't need to know any of that.

"I understand what you're saying, sir," I replied. "All I can say is I'm sorry and I'll never leave either of them again."

"Sorry doesn't mean anything, unless you mean it," he said. "And at this point, it's not enough for me."

I watched as Marcus turned back to Regan's room, leaving me there leaning on the wall like a dick. Well, fuck. Now what do I do?

I followed behind Marcus and entered Regan's room to see her and Rory cuddled up together. Rory had her eyes closed and Regan was holding her, smoothing her hair back from her face as she slept. I smiled at Regan, loving how she had taken such good care of our precious little cub. I was still amazed that this was real. When I spoke to Trevor to warn him of Janet's plans, all I had planned was to be able to leave town with a clear conscious. I now had more than I had ever dreamed. I had Regan and I had Rory. I had everything I could have ever wanted. I couldn't wait to get my girls home, where we could begin to be a real family.

"Regan, are you ready to go home?" Marcus asked. "I've got your things here so you can get ready to go."

Marcus pointedly ignored my presence in the room, which at this point wasn't a bad thing. I could feel the animosity coming from him as he spoke to Regan. I was sure she could feel the tension too but was staying quiet about it.

The nurse came back in and helped Regan up to go into the attached bathroom and assisted her in getting cleaned up and dressed. While she was in there, Rory sat with Marcus, occasionally looking over at me in confusion then going back to playing an imaginary game with her grandfather. It was funny to watch, that was for sure.

Regan came back out of the bathroom within minutes, dressed in jeans and a light blue tee shirt. She looked amazing, considering she'd been in an explosion only a week before. She was still bruised up, but her broken bones were healing nicely.

We waited for the doctor to come in and give us Regan's release papers, then we headed out of the hospital. We got to my car, and as I was about to ask Regan if she would ride with me, Marcus spoke up and said,

"Regan, I've got the car seat for Rory. Let's go in the truck, sunshine."

Regan looked over at me to gauge my reaction, I'm sure. I waved her off towards her dad's truck with a smile, calling over the roof of my car,

"No worries, darling. I'll see you there."

Marcus glared at me for several minutes before shaking his head. He helped Rory into her seat, buckling her belts and then getting into the truck. Starting the engine, he waited for Regan to get in and close her door. She turned and smiled over at me and then climbed in, closing her door. Her dad took off and left the parking lot heading for the family compound. I followed behind him until we reached the turnoff for the compound. Once we were inside the gates, I pulled up near what was once the main meeting building. I still couldn't fathom what the hell Janet had been thinking, blowing up a damn building, hurting my mate in the process. Someone could have been killed. She never was one for thinking ahead.

Marcus shoved his door open and stomped over to where I was standing waiting for Regan. I was glad she couldn't hear what was said but I knew she could tell they were angry words on her dad's side. I watched as Marcus cocked his fist and let it fly, hitting me in the nose, which was still bruised from my run in with Trevor. I winced as I tilted my head back to stop the blood flow that was running freely down onto my shirt.

I watched as Regan gingerly exited her father's truck and headed over to where I was standing, leaning against the bumper of my car. She stopped in front of me and laced her arms around my waist, laying her head on my shoulder, where she gave a deep sigh.

"What's wrong, baby?" I asked her.

"Nothing's wrong," she replied, but there was something in her voice that said that something was definitely wrong.

I stroked her back as she held on to me tightly and lightly rubbed her cheek on my shirt. I reveled in the feeling of having her in my arms again.

"Baby, are you going to introduce me to Rory?" I asked quietly, hoping to keep her father from hearing me. I was pretty sure they'd had words on the way here.

"Yes, right now, if you want," she replied, looking up at me with a smile.

"I'd like that a lot," I said.

"Love doesn't always make sense, but when it does, it's magic..."

Chapter Thirteen

Regan

I looked back over my shoulder, smiled at Johnny, and then got into the truck with my dad. I knew they had talked in the hallway, although it wasn't a very long conversation. My dad was upset about the whole thing, and I could tell that this was going to be a long drive home by the way he was grinding his teeth.

"Regan, that's the man who left you to have Rory alone?" Marcus asked angrily.

"Yes, that's Johnny, Rory's father," I answered him softly.

"Why didn't he stay?" my dad questioned further. "When he found out about Rory and that you were mates?"

"He didn't know about Rory, Dad," I replied. "I never told him I was pregnant. I didn't want him to feel trapped, and at the time, I thought he was just happy to hang with that bunch of idiots that followed Hatchet."

"And now?" he asked me. "Is he still following that bunch of idiots?"

"Daddy, there was a reason he was there," I said on a sigh, "but I can't discuss it with you. Suffice it to say, the clan is no longer a problem between us, and not just because Janet is dead and gone."

"That's good, but I still think he's an asshat for leaving his mate," Dad said. "And he's going to have to work to make it up to you and to that amazing baby girl napping in the backseat."

"Dad, he doesn't need to make it up to us. He just needs to be in this with me the whole way," I replied. I was starting to get steamed. I understood my dad's point of view; I did. I just wished he'd keep it to himself. We drove up to the compound and Dad pushed the button on his dash to open the outer gate. We drove through and pulled up to our cabin. I looked over at my dad. I could see the concern on his face, the anger in his eyes, and I knew at some point, there was going to be a confrontation. My dad was the sweetest man, but he was also a very dominant grizzly bear.

Dad shoved his door open and stomped over to where Johnny stood waiting for me. I couldn't hear what was said but I could tell they were angry words on my dad's side. I watched as my dad cocked his fist and let it fly, hitting Johnny in the nose, which was still bruised from his run in with Trevor. I winced as Johnny tilted his head back to stop the blood flow that was running freely down onto his shirt.

I watched Johnny for several moments then walked over. I stopped in front of him and laced my arms around his waist, laying my head on his shoulder, I gave a deep sigh and then took a deep breath in to capture his scent. I stood like that for what seemed like hours, but in reality, was only minutes. He held me and stroked my back up and down in a soothing gesture. I missed this, being able to just be with him. Hold him in my arms and just be.

"What's wrong baby?" Johnny asked.

"Nothing's wrong," I replied, but there was something wrong; my dad had just given me the third degree when it came to Johnny's and my relationship.

Johnny stroked my back as I held onto him tightly and rubbed my cheek on his shirt. I loved the feeling of being able to just hold him if I wanted. Johnny looked at me with nervousness in his eyes. I knew this would be hard for him, as he'd missed so much. But I knew we were going to change that right now.

"Baby, are you going to introduce me to Rory?" he asked me quietly.

"Yes, right now, if you want," I replied, looking up at him with a smile.

"I'd like that a lot," he said.

I took his hand and lead him to the small playground. I gave a slight push when we got to the bench we had installed.

"I'll be right back," I told him. "Don't go anywhere."

"I won't," he replied. "I'll be right here waiting."

I walked towards the house, entering the kitchen. I gave my dad 'the look.' You know, the one that says 'don't mess with me'.
Walking slowly down the hall toward my room, I daydreamed of what our lives would be like now. Now that Rory's dad was in our lives. I dreamed of our claiming, becoming one. I came to my door. Quietly pushing it open, I saw Rory still curled on one side, her eyes open and bright. She saw me too. Calling to me, she stood in her crib and raised her arms, saying,

"Mama, up!"

I picked up my sweet girl and cuddled her to me, breathing in her sweet baby scent. I walked back to the kitchen and out the back door, heading back to the play area where I had left Johnny waiting.

"Rory, baby, there's someone I want you to meet," I said to the light of my life. "This is your daddy."

Rory lifted her head and gazed into Johnny's eyes in awe, eyes so like hers. I could see the colors swirl as they looked at each other. Rory smiled her little mischievous smile and then reaching her arms towards Johnny, she said,

"Daddy, up."

My girl knew just what to do to melt her daddy's heart. I watched Johnny, a bigger than life, full grown grizzly male, take his little girl in his arms and through a watery smile, he said,

"Hey, peanut. Sorry I'm late."

Rory looked at her daddy and said,
"It's ok, daddy," making us both laugh out loud.

Johnny sat back on the bench and held our girl on his lap, almost like he was afraid she'd disappear if he wasn't holding her. I sat beside them and gave a happy sigh. Rory started to squirm, her attention captured by the swing set that was just beyond where we were sitting together. Johnny let her down and she toddled over and got into the small swinging seat we'd added when the babies were able to walk and climb on their own. Watching our little girl act as if the appearance of her dad was an everyday expected occurrence made me realize that this was turning out to be one of the best days of our lives together. And it could only get better from here.

Johnny took my hand in his and raised it to his lips, gently placing a kiss on my palm. He gave my fingers a little squeeze, let me go, and wandered over to push our little girl on the swings. Sweetest sight ever right there.

"Where there is hope,

there is love..."

Chapter Fourteen
Johnny

I watched as my little girl played and laughed, knowing this was the start to the rest of my life. I would protect Rory and Regan to my last breath for the rest of my life. This is what was most important. I just forgot along the way. My mom used to say where there is hope, there is love. And that's so true, but I also believe that where there is love, there is hope and a future. A future for us all to be together and know that we are forever.

We watched Rory play for several more minutes, then Regan called her over so that we could go inside. It was getting late, and we were all hungry.

We walked hand in hand into the cabin, Rory perched on Regan's hip, chattering away and all smiles. Once inside, Regan set Rory in her high chair and started to assemble sandwiches for us to eat. I watched both of my girls, happy for the first time in a long time, since before my parents and siblings had died at the hands of Hatchet and his gang of bears that were only out for themselves.

Regan finished the sandwiches and put them on plates, along with chips and some salad made with what looked like rabbit food. I don't really do vegetables but for her, I'd eat every bite.

As we ate, we talked of what was, what is and what would be. We spoke of the day at the pond when she had to make the best decision for herself and our cub. It was still a raw wound, but I could understand why. No one wants their family in danger, and I definitely didn't want them on Hatchet's or Janet's radar back then.

We spoke of the explosion that had sent her to the hospital. I still didn't know how they had gotten the explosives so close to the clan building, and Ian was still investigating the area to see if they could figure out who wanted them distracted that day, besides Janet and the others who had decided to attack Trevor and his mate.

And then we had the discussion that would change our lives, bind us together through thick and thin.

"Babe, I know we need to take it slow," I said, "but I need you to know, I am all in on this life."

Regan watched me for several seconds, an unreadable look in her eyes. She then replied,

"I'm all in too, and I don't really want to wait. We've waited long enough. Don't you think?"

"I couldn't agree more, beautiful," I said with a smile. Pulling her from the chair at the table, I wrapped her in my arms and brought my lips to hers, sealing the bargain that we'd just made. On a sigh, I let her go. Rory was still sitting in the kitchen with us and who knew where Marcus had gotten to. I kissed her once more, this time a kiss filled with promise for when we were alone.

Laughing, she pulled away from me and started to clean up the mess Rory had made of herself and of the floor. Cute didn't even begin to describe the look on her face when Regan wiped her down with a damp towel. She looked so disgusted and with a small squawk of annoyance, she lifted her arms and demanded,

"Down."

I knew this behavior was going to be an issue, but she was so adorable, and I had just gotten her in my life. Learning curve, for sure. I lifted her from her chair and kissed her cheek, letting her down on the floor. She toddled off towards the living room.

Regan finished clean up and then we both followed after Rory. Hand in hand, I couldn't get enough contact. It was like I was afraid that she would disappear or this was all just a dream. Unsure of where we would be staying, I took a moment to gather my thoughts and then began,

"Baby, I think we need to talk about what we're going to do, don't you?"

"I think so too," Regan replied.

"This is what I am thinking," I said. "I want us to live together and be together. What kind of timeline are we talking about?"

"Timeline?" she asked. "For what?"

"Our mating, being together forever," I replied, starting to think I had misread the way she was feeling.

"Oh, no. No timeline. We are doing that as soon as Lauren gets here. I called her a little while ago, and she is going to come get Rory for a slumber party with the twins," she answered. "And my dad has left for a few days. He said he had some things to do."

Oh man, how did I get so lucky, I thought to myself. A babysitter and her dad had given us space. So many thoughts were running through my head, but how to let her know that I would love her forever was at the forefront of my mind. I didn't want there to ever be any doubt between us.

"Babe, that's the best news I've heard all day," I said with a smile just as someone knocked on the door.

"Come in," Regan called out.

"Hey lady, are you ready for me to take your little terror off your hands for a while?" Lauren said as she walked through the front door. She smiled and waved at me and then went to where Rory was playing. Bending down to her, Lauren said, "Are you ready to go visit the boys, sweetie?"

"Go, let's go," Rory answered with a laugh. I watched the by play with a certain amount of awe. You could tell that our little girl was loved by everyone when they interacted with her. It was obvious in their words and their actions. It was a wonderful feeling, knowing that she had been taken care of.

"Thank you for taking her," Regan said. "I appreciate it."

"I'm sure you do," Lauren replied with a giggle. "Do you have her bag ready?"

"It's by the door. I'll walk with you to your place," Regan answered.

"Cool. Let's go, Bug," Lauren said to Rory.
Rory toddled over and grabbed Lauren's hand.
Looking at me, she said,

"You go too, daddy?"

"Yep, I'll go too, sweetheart," I answered, taking
her little hand in mine as we walked out the door
followed by Lauren and Regan. When we got to
Ian and Lauren's cabin, Rory ran inside with a
small wave and 'bye' to go see what the boys
were up to. We handed off Rory's bag of overnight
things and said our goodbyes.

On the walk back to the cabin, we strolled slowly
across the open yard. Looking off to the right, I
could see what was left of the burnt out building,
and squeezing Regan's hand, I shuddered a little
thinking of how close I had come to losing her,
losing them both. When we got to the cabin door,
Regan led me through into the house, down the
hall and into her bedroom. Stopping at the closed
door, she peered at me over her shoulder.

"Are we sure we want to do this?" she asked
tentatively. I was surprised, as my Regan wasn't
the tentative type.

"I'm sure," I answered. "Are you?"

She smiled at me, pulled me through the door of
her bedroom and said,

"So sure."

I followed her like a puppy, happy to be in her presence. As we cleared the doorway, she gave a small yank on my hand, closing the door once I was clear. I breathed in, longing to imprint her scent on my memory, wanting that connection with her on so many levels. Once the door was closed, she turned to me and looked up into my eyes. I could see the lust in her eyes, the love and the beginnings of the trust she used to give me so freely before I fucked it all up with my choices. I needed to feel her again, in my arms writhing beneath me or riding the waves of pleasure as she rode my cock. That was one of our favorite positions, and I couldn't wait to be reintroduced to her body after so long of being apart.

"Johnny, I think we need to lose these clothes," she said playfully as she ran her hands to the button on my jeans, slowly unhooking it and then easing the zipper down. Once my pants were undone, she ran her hands around my waist and into my boxers. Her hands slowly traveling over my ass and back up to the small of my back. While she explored my rear end, I took the opportunity to run my hands up her shirt where I found her breasts on full display, no bra. This was so my day. I tenderly ran one hand over her left breast, teasing her nipple into a stiff peak. I took my hands back out of her shirt and ran my hands to the hem of it, lifting slowly while moving in to give her a scorching hot kiss. I took her shirt up and over her head, baring her breasts to my eyes. On a moan, I leaned in and took her stiff left nipple into my waiting mouth, suckling and licking, drawing a groan of pleasure from her throat. The whole time, she continued to run her hands up and down my back to my ass. While I nibbled and tasted her peak, my hand went to her right breast, where I continued to torment her with a slight twisting motion on her breast and nipple. Taking my thumb and forefinger, I gave a slight twisting pinch and she groaned again. She began to walk backwards toward her bed, and I followed, continuing my assault on her breasts, loving the moans that were coming from her throat with each twist and each lick of my tongue. When we got to the bed, she pulled away from me, making me stop my worship of her tits. She took my shirt into her hands and whipped it over my head. She then took both hands at the hips of my jeans and pushed them down along with my boxers to the floor. I stepped out of my pants, leaning back in for another kiss, all tongue and teeth, my favorite feeling in the world. Well, my second favorite feeling, with the first being when I sank my cock into her tight pussy and worked her open to take my girth. I had always had to work her a little each time; no matter how many times we made love, she was always just as tight as the last time.

I slowly worked her leggings off. When they were to her knees, I dropped to the floor and just stared.

I had missed her but I'd also missed her pussy. I dove for it like an Olympic diver off the high board, pulling her hips to me. I tongued her lips apart and went as deep as I could, causing Regan to drag in a startled breath. As I licked her core, with a little pressure from my probing tongue and a little help of my fingers on her clit, she began to rub her pussy on my face, slow at first and then she picked up speed. As I got her off with my tongue and fingers, I could feel her pussy weeping with excitement, which only caused me to lick her faster, deeper, and harder. My fingers slowly pinched her clit, and she exploded on my face with a rush of liquid that I lapped up like a dehydrated pup. I loved every second of her orgasm. I continued to lick up her essence until she slumped and stopped humping into my mouth. I kissed my way up her belly to her breasts, stopping to leave a wet kiss on each one. I then got off the floor and laid her on the bed, covering her body with mine. My hard on was so stiff that it was like a sword poking into the mattress between her legs.

"Baby, I am gonna make you do that again," I said cockily.

"I know you will," she replied with a spent smile. "I can't wait either."

As she was speaking, she was slowly moving, causing my dick to insert into her pussy at a shallow depth and I wanted more, so much more, and I wanted deeper. On one upward thrust I seated myself into heaven on earth, and her pussy clutched at my dick as I worked her. Another inward thrust with a slow retreat, almost all the way out and then a quick inward thrust again. As we moved together, her breathing increased, and my body was slick with sweat. Her hands were clutching my ass, pulling me into her deeper. With each thrust, I was hitting her cervix.

"Oh, God!" she cried out, "Yes, Johnny, yes!"

I reveled in her calling me Johnny. Finally she was able to exclaim her pleasure and my bear was happy that she could use our real name at last. I thrust into her again as she rubbed herself on my dick. I could feel my balls begin to churn, and it was only a matter of time before I would cum. I worked her a little longer, enjoying the sounds and movements she was making. As I plunged into her depths, I kissed my way to the pulse in her neck. Pausing, I pulled from her and looked into her eyes, saying,

"Are you sure this is what you want, love?"

"Do it. I can't wait to be yours," she answered as she had her second orgasm of our claiming.

With that, I could feel my face elongate and my teeth lengthen. With one last powerful drive, I let my teeth pierce her skin at the same time as she did the same, and in that moment, we claimed each other, becoming one, forever. As I felt our souls mingle, I gave one more deep thrust, holding myself in her pussy and letting loose, cum spurting from my cock into her pussy and coating her cervix. She began to slow her movements. I could feel her inner walls milking the last of my cum from my balls. She licked the wound on my neck from our claiming, causing me to shiver in pleasure. I knew that nothing would ever drive us apart. This was forever.

"Baby, you are the best," I said on a sigh as I held myself in her depths and looked into her love glazed eyes. "I love you, you know."

"I love you more than life," she replied as she began to giggle up at me.

"What's so funny?" I asked in confusion.

"You and the look on your face right now. It's hilarious," she said. "You look like you've been whacked up side the head and are all dazed."

"Baby, that is exactly how I feel," I said. "But I know just what happened here. We became one -- you, me, and our cub."

The look that came over her face had me worried for a moment. She looked like she was going to cry, so I stroked her hair back from her face and kissed her softly. We were still connected in the most intimate way, and I could feel my cock filling once more.

Regan locked her leg over my hip and flipped us over, so she was sitting up proudly looking down to where we were still joined. She began to rock back and forth, picking up speed and making me moan in pleasure. I never wanted this to end. The feeling of her riding my dick was almost too good. I pushed up into her as she rocked again, making her gasp loudly. She started to move up and down my cock, but as she pulled up, she would tighten her inner muscles and then slide down slowly until I was balls deep. She would then hold herself to me and then pull back off again. At this point, she lost all rhythm and started to bounce on my dick like she was on a bumpy gravel road, and the feeling was amazing. I flipped us again to where she was lying on her back. She looked up into my eyes and whispered,

"Do it again."

I knew exactly what she wanted. Picking up speed, I pushed into her harder and then said,

"Touch yourself, baby. Bring us home."

She ran her hand down to her clit and began to rub in fast little circles. I could feel the fluttering of her pussy that signaled her impending orgasm. I could feel my own orgasm start as my balls tightened and then I felt Regan spasm and cum, which triggered my own release. As I emptied myself into her, I nipped at her claim mark, causing her pussy to tighten even further. My dick felt like it was in a vise, the pressure so good that I continued to cum, three more spurts and I was spent. I collapsed to the side, making sure not to flatten her to the bed with my weight.

"Baby, I am gonna do that to you everyday, forever," I told her in a gasping breath.

"I'll hold you to that," she laughingly replied.

We spent the rest of the afternoon in bed, then together we showered and had a repeat performance up against the tile wall. Slippery but so satisfying.

We got dressed and headed for the kitchen after our shower to refuel. As we sat down to eat, I looked at Regan and said,

"Can we go get Rory, babe? I love being here with you, but I would really like to get to know our daughter."

"Oh, babe. Of course," she said. "I just wanted you to myself for our claiming."

"I have found the love of a lifetime..."

Chapter Fifteen
Regan

I gazed over at Johnny and thought life couldn't get any better than this. I watched the man that I loved, the father of our child, looking at me with love in his eyes and a satisfied smile on his face. I looked at him and knew the Fates had been kind, giving me the man that I needed and wanted, all rolled into one. As I stood staring at him, he looked up at me and said,

"Can we go get Rory, babe? I love being here with you, but I would really like to get to know our daughter."

"Oh, babe. Of course," I said. "I just wanted you to myself for our claiming."

I grabbed on to his hand and we headed for Ian and Lauren's cabin to get our precious little cub. After gathering her things and telling Lauren, Ian, and the twins goodnight, we headed back to the cabin and settled in for a night of cuddles and smooches from our Rory.

We fell asleep in a huddle of hugs, arms and legs intertwined, Johnny and my soul woven together, Rory snug between us. When the morning light reflected through the bedroom window, we all woke with a yawn and good stretch. I looked at my little family and smiled a contented smile. I was happy that we were a family, finally after so long. We could now raise our little bean and maybe have more children. You never know what life has in store for you.

What I did know is that I had finally found the love of a lifetime, my forever. Johnny and I were one, Fated Mates. This was all I'd ever wanted and all I'd ever needed.

I hoped my dad could see what a wonderful man Johnny is, now that he knows that family is the most important thing, that putting your mate and child first isn't a mistake but a blessing. Because love is a blessing, something to hold onto with both hands and work at, relationships are hard but as Fated Mates we could make this work for a lifetime...

Forever.

Thank you for reading my first series, Bears in Love. Stay tuned for my next series, which will follow the next generation as they find their happily ever after... Coming soon!

You can find more information about all of my books, my crazy days and join in on some fun shenanigans by following me on Facebook and Twitter.

www.facebook.com/pa.vachonauthor.33

https://twitter.com/PAvachonauthor

All the love and smooches!

Made in the USA
Columbia, SC
26 September 2023